Conte[nts]

Garrick Green Infant School, Garrick Green

Josh Paylor (6)	1
Rory Caley (7)	2
Monica Raviraj (7)	3
Harvey Breeze (7)	4
Keira Frosdick (6)	5
Jessica Jolly (6)	6
Ashley Brennan (6)	7
Declan Cooper (7)	8
Phoebe Sanders (7)	9
Lewis Scantlebury (7)	10
William Houghton (7)	11
Jasmine Hewitt (7)	12

Greenacre First & Middle School, Great Yarmouth

Charlie Bowler	13
Nazi Ali (7)	14
Chardanai Woodhouse (7)	15
Jessica Prendi (7)	16
Stephanie Watson	17
Brett Fransham (7)	18
Kayleigh Parker (7)	19
Scott Medley (7)	20
Bailey Wilson (7)	21
Rhys Rowen (7)	22
Paige Surgeoner (7)	23
Michal Tondryk (7)	24
Charlie Price	25
Luke Crowe (7)	26
Paige Medley (7)	27
Kaitlyn Cooper (7)	28
Connor Gill (7)	29
Michael Brown (7)	30
Raphael Ejaz (7)	31
Sasha Hill (7)	32
Shannon Grant (7)	33
Alan Hancock (7)	34
Jakub Mazierz (6)	35

Bethany Colley (7)	
Joshua Richardson (6)	37
Owen Banyard (7)	38
Chloe Bullen (6)	39
Jack Flett (7)	40
Alfie Crown (7)	41
Taylor Everitt (7)	42
Charlotte Colclough (6)	43
Gabrielle Colclough (6)	44
Saffron Swalwell (6)	45
Adele Eke (7)	46
Isabel Overton (7)	47
Briony Benjamin (7)	48
Alice Zelepukina (6)	49
Alice Middleton-Jones (6)	50
Alicia Rolfe (6)	51
Riley Berycz (6)	52
Rebecca Ward (7)	53
Erin Lanchester (6)	54

Meadow CP School, Lowestoft

Ellie-Mai Crawford (6)	55
Sarah Beattie (7)	56
Tayla Hayward (6)	57
Emma Henwood (7)	58
Eleanor Manning (6)	59
Tegan Arlow (7)	60
Amy Clark (6)	61
Callum Westphal (7)	62
Wilym Dunnell (6)	63
Sophie Bush (6)	64
Natalie Raven (6)	65
Riley Higgins (7)	66
Kensey Wigg (7)	67
Morgan Gallagher (7)	68
Annie Angus (7)	69
Isabel Fields (7)	70
Abbie-Beth Beharier (7)	71
Megan Sampson (7)	72
Rebecca Casbolt (7)	73
Neo Beck (7)	74

Ipswich Preparatory School, Ipswich

William Parsons (5) 75
Caitlin Wood (4) 76
Naomi De Silva (5) 77
Jy Naha (4) 78
Lucy Procter (5) 79
George Lewis (4) 80
Angus Williams (5) 81
Monty Brown (5) 82
Laura Tickle (4) 83
Harry Budd (5) 84
Jensen Hoole (5) 85
Thomas Licence (5) 86
Lia Fletcher (4) 87
Charlotte Pudney (4) 88
Varun Sharma (5) 89
Maddison Taylor (5) 90
Adam Rudolph (5) 91
Matthew Daly (4) 92
Brylle Ibasco (4) 93
Joella Kajoba (5) 94
Harvey Ormes (5) 95
Etiane Cheung (4) 96
Toby Jermyn (5) 97
Joshua Midwood (5) 98
Joseph Breheny (4) 99
Bethan Cherry (5) 100
Megan Bureau (5) 101
Alexander Mair (5) 102
Eve McCallum (5) 103
Helena Marfoh-Gillings (5) 104
Muskaan Sethi (6) 105
Charlie Parsons (5) 106
Harry Dunnett (5) 107
Sophie Reeves-Croft (6) 108
Harry Roper (5) 109
Samuel Burgoyne (6) 110
Jack Aggett (6) 111
Saba Behnia (5) 112
Anna Van Staden (6) 113
James Whittle (6) 114
Oliver O'Brien (6) 115
Francesca Rogers (6) 116
Charlie Coe (6) 117
Joseph Christie (6) 118
Sophie Garner (5) 119

Tabitha Creed (5) 120
Francis Gorham (6) 121
Samuel Duncombe (6) 122
William Reed (6) 123
Oliver Cook (5) 124
Tom Conway (6) 125
Aiden Pearson (5) 126
Ryan Goodarzi (6) 127

Langham Village School, Norfolk

Rosie Valentine (7) 128
Teddy Valentine (7) 129
Connor McInally (7) 130
Lily Everard (7) 131
Bethany Everitt (7) 132
Maisie Moxon (6) 133
Blue Wilson (7) 134

Middleton CP School, Middleton

Erin Pain (5) 135
Ian Simpson (6) 136
Saffron Jackson (6) 137
David Lloyd (6) 138
Thomas Marshall (6) 139
Hebe Cooke (6) 140
Layla Brown (7) 141
Gabriella Pattinson (7) 142
Cameron Berry (7) 143
Mollie Shaw (7) 144

Redcastle Furze Primary School, Thetford

Todd Middleton (5) 145
Kiran Manir (6) 146
Alex Knock (5) 147
Paydon Blow (5) 148
Kira Baumane (5) 149
Harry Brown (5) 150
Ricardo Da Silva (6) 151
Bruno Cardoso (6) 152
Codie Ancliff (6) 153
Katharine Mold (6) 154
Natasha Laurie (6) 155
Andrew Souness (6) 156

Runcton Holme CE Primary School, Runcton Holme

Daniel Turner (6) 157

Lucie Canham (6) 158
Grace Herbert (5) 159
Reece Hockton (6) 160
Amber Nederpel (6) 161
Emily Shimmin (6) 162
Olivia Ward (6) 163

Sacred Heart Convent School, Swaffham
Elizabeth Napper (7) 164
Isobel McPartlin (6) 165
Emily Harpham-Wells (7) 166
Alice Christian (7) 167
Charlotte MacEwan (6) 168
Áine Matthews (7) 169

Tattingstone CE (VCP) School, Tattingstone
Alexander Wrathall (5) 170
Michael Vinnicombe (6) 171
Lucy Sweeney (6) 172
Morgan Porter (6) 173
Joseph Moore (5) 174
Richard Marsh (6) 175
Jake Henson (6) 176
Esme Chancellor (5) 177
Phoebe Agar (6) 178

Wenhaston Primary School, Wenhaston
Harry Leeming (7) 179
Jamie Lea Stacey (7) 180
George Curtis (6) 181
Jake McMaster (7) 182
Kiaya Cooke (6) 183
Olivia Smithers (7) 184

Yoxford Primary School, Yoxford
Bethany Constance (6) 185
Harry Nichols (7) 186
Ryan Southey (6) 187
Oscar Phillips (6) 188
Maisie Beckett (6) 189
Jaydon Johnson (5) 190
Cameron Cutler (5) 191
Luke Clarke (5) 192
Jacob Last (7) 193
Dylan Corbett (6) 194

My First Acrostic

Norfolk & Suffolk

Edited by Aimée Vanstone

First published in Great Britain in 2009 by:

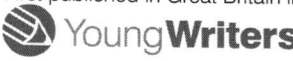 Young**Writers**

Young Writers
Remus House
Coltsfoot Drive
Peterborough
PE2 9JX
Telephone: 01733 890066
Website: www.youngwriters.co.uk

All Rights Reserved
© Copyright Contributors 2009
SB ISBN 978-1-84924-374-2

Foreword

The 'My First Acrostic' collection was developed by Young Writers specifically for Key Stage 1 children. The poetic form is simple, fun and gives the young poet a guideline to shape their ideas, yet at the same time leaves room for their imagination and creativity to begin to blossom.

Due to the young age of the entrants we have enjoyed rewarding their effort by including as many of the poems as possible. Our hope is that seeing their work in print will encourage the children to grow and develop their writing skills to become our poets of tomorrow.

Young Writers has been publishing children's poetry for over 19 years. Our aim is to nurture creativity in our children and young adults, to give them an interest in poetry and an outlet to express themselves. This latest collection will act as a milestone for the young poets and one that will be enjoyable to revisit again and again.

The Poems

My First Acrostic - Norfolk & Suffolk

Joshie

J ellies all the time
O ctober starts me being clever
S houts when I'm very, very, very cross!
H ave lots and lots of friends, more than 27
I like carrots and pasta!
E njoys 8th May, my birthday!

Josh Paylor (6)
Garrick Green Infant School, Garrick Green

Rory Caley

R eads lots of books
O rdinary boy
R eady for anything
Y ummy foods

C heese is my favourite food
A mazing
L emur is my favourite animal
E xciting
Y ellow is my favourite colour.

Rory Caley (7)
Garrick Green Infant School, Garrick Green

My First Acrostic - Norfolk & Suffolk

Monica

M ops the floor for Mum.
O range is my best fruit.
N ever leaves the light on.
I n the shops I like to buy veg.
C hips are my favourite food.
A pple crumble is my best pie.

Monica Raviraj (7)
Garrick Green Infant School, Garrick Green

Harvey

H ard-working
A ctive
R ads and writes lots of books
V acuums a lot
E nergetic
Y ellow is my favourite colour.

Harvey Breeze (7)
Garrick Green Infant School, Garrick Green

My First Acrostic - Norfolk & Suffolk

Keira

K ind to people
E yes that are blue
I like ginger beer
R unning is my best sport
A nd tennis is fun.

Keira Frosdick (6)
Garrick Green Infant School, Garrick Green

Jessica

July is when I have my birthday.
Easter is my favourite time of year.
Some people like me.
Sometimes I like making models.
Ice is very hard for me to walk on.
Card is my favourite type of paper.
Activities are what I like doing.

Jessica Jolly (6)
Garrick Green Infant School, Garrick Green

My First Acrostic - Norfolk & Suffolk

Ashley Brennan

A shley, I'm 6 years old.
S easides are my favourite place.
H esitate when arguing.
L oves music.
E yes are blue and green.
Y oghurt is yum.

B old writing.
R ealistic.
E aster eggs are yum.
N athan is my bro.
N athan is fast.
A manda is my mum.
N athan is strong.

Ashley Brennan (6)
Garrick Green Infant School, Garrick Green

Declan

D ifferent
E lephant is my favourite animal
C ooper is my second name
L amb is my best thing for tea
A chocolate pudding is my favourite pudding
N ight-time I like playing with my Wii.

Declan Cooper (7)
Garrick Green Infant School, Garrick Green

My First Acrostic - Norfolk & Suffolk

Phoebe Sanders

P retty hair.
H orses are my favourite animals.
O rdinary.
E aster is my second favourite time of year.
B eautiful clothes.
E aster eggs are yummy scrummy.

S easides are my favourite places.
A ndrew is my uncle.
N eptune is my favourite planet.
D ifferent.
E nergetic.
R ealistic.
S ausages are tasty.

Phoebe Sanders (7)
Garrick Green Infant School, Garrick Green

Lewis

L ewis is 7
E ats chocolate a lot!
W ins games
I love red
S miles a lot.

Lewis Scantlebury (7)
Garrick Green Infant School, Garrick Green

My First Acrostic - Norfolk & Suffolk

William

W ins games
I nteresting boy
L ions are my favourite animal
L ikes Dr Pepper
I am good at football
A m good at writing
M y favourite colour is black.

William Houghton (7)
Garrick Green Infant School, Garrick Green

Jasmine

J ust very rich.
A n excellent worker.
S ilent and peaceful.
M y favourite animal is a dolphin.
I 'm funny.
N ever brush my teeth.
E at McDonald's.

Jasmine Hewitt (7)
Garrick Green Infant School, Garrick Green

My First Acrostic - Norfolk & Suffolk

Charlie

C heeky smile
H appy
A boy
R uns fast
L oud
I ncredible
E xcited.

Charlie Bowler
Greenacre First & Middle School, Great Yarmouth

Nazi Ali

N ice
A nimal
Z ooming
I ncredible

A mazes
L ikeable
I ndividual.

Nazi Ali (7)
Greenacre First & Middle School, Great Yarmouth

My First Acrostic - Norfolk & Suffolk

Chardanai

C uddly
H appy
A lovely girl
R eading is good
D reaming of flowers
A nd
N ever like
A nts
I love my family.

Chardanai Woodhouse (7)
Greenacre First & Middle School, Great Yarmouth

Jessica

J elly is yummy
E ating
S paghetti is yummy
S o is a banana
I love cats
C limbing is fun
A pples are yum.

Jessica Prendi (7)
Greenacre First & Middle School, Great Yarmouth

My First Acrostic - Norfolk & Suffolk

Stephanie

S unny days.
T aping people on their video camera.
E ating.
P ainting.
H iding.
A nimals.
N ot like rainy days.
I love my mummy.
E ggs and soldiers.

Stephanie Watson
Greenacre First & Middle School, Great Yarmouth

Brett

B iking
R eally good at climbing
E ating
T ickling
T icklish.

Brett Fransham (7)
Greenacre First & Middle School, Great Yarmouth

My First Acrostic - Norfolk & Suffolk

Kayleigh

K ind
A mazing
Y oung
L ovely
E xcellent
I ntelligent
G reat
H appy.

Kayleigh Parker (7)
Greenacre First & Middle School, Great Yarmouth

Scott

S uper
C aring
O riginal
T errific
T idy.

Scott Medley (7)
Greenacre First & Middle School, Great Yarmouth

My First Acrostic - Norfolk & Suffolk

Bailey

B rave
A mazing
I ntelligent
L ike looking at books
E nergetic
Y es I'm me.

Bailey Wilson (7)
Greenacre First & Middle School, Great Yarmouth

Rhys

R eally nice
H appy
Y ou're unique
S neaky.

Rhys Rowen (7)
Greenacre First & Middle School, Great Yarmouth

My First Acrostic - Norfolk & Suffolk

Paige

P ersonal
A mazing
I ncredible
G reat
E xcellent.

Paige Surgeoner (7)
Greenacre First & Middle School, Great Yarmouth

Michal

M y puppy is funny
I love my puppy
C ircus is my favourite
H unting is my favourite
A nimals are my favourite
L ove my mum.

Michal Tondryk (7)
Greenacre First & Middle School, Great Yarmouth

My First Acrostic - Norfolk & Suffolk

Charlie

C harlie sometimes
H appy sometimes
A ngry likes
R ed sometimes
L onely but he
I s
E xcellent.

Charlie Price
Greenacre First & Middle School, Great Yarmouth

Luke

L ike sweets
U se my brain in maths
K ind and helpful
E ars good for listening.

Luke Crowe (7)
Greenacre First & Middle School, Great Yarmouth

My First Acrostic - Norfolk & Suffolk

Paige

P erfect at writing
A lways good at behaving
I love my mum
G ood at looking after my cat
E ats bananas.

Paige Medley (7)
Greenacre First & Middle School, Great Yarmouth

Kaitlyn

K aitlyn
A lovely girl
I am lovely
T errific
L ike eating food
Y es oranges
N ot tomatoes.

Kaitlyn Cooper (7)
Greenacre First & Middle School, Great Yarmouth

My First Acrostic - Norfolk & Suffolk

Connor

C onnor is a boy.
O n a bike I'm fast.
N ot a girl.
N ot a food.
O n my PS2 I am good.
R ide a skateboard, I'm fast.

Connor Gill (7)
Greenacre First & Middle School, Great Yarmouth

Michael Brown

M an
I ncredible
C old
H e
A mazing
E njoys and
L aughs.

Michael Brown (7)
Greenacre First & Middle School, Great Yarmouth

My First Acrostic - Norfolk & Suffolk

Raphael

R ight
A lready
P erfect at running
H appy
A good boy
E xcellent
L ikes playing.

Raphael Ejaz (7)
Greenacre First & Middle School, Great Yarmouth

Sasha Hill

S unny
A nimal
S uper
H appy
A mazing.

Sasha Hill (7)
Greenacre First & Middle School, Great Yarmouth

My First Acrostic - Norfolk & Suffolk

Shannon

S ometimes I am
H appy
A nd
N ever
N ever
O ver
N ight.

Shannon Grant (7)
Greenacre First & Middle School, Great Yarmouth

Alan

A smiley boy
L ikes to eat an apple
A s fast as a runner
N ot a girl.

Alan Hancock (7)
Greenacre First & Middle School, Great Yarmouth

Jakub

𝕁 olly
𝔸 ctive
𝕂 ind
𝕌 nderstanding
𝔹 rave.

Jakub Mazierz (6)
Greenacre First & Middle School, Great Yarmouth

Bethany

B ananas are tasty
E ggs are my favourite food
T asty food that I like
H ugs when I go to bed
A pples are juicy
N ever eats cakes
Y oghurts are sweet.

Bethany Colley (7)
Greyfriars Primary School, King's Lynn

My First Acrostic - Norfolk & Suffolk

Josh

J ogging the football
O ranges are juicy
S andwich lover
H oney.

Joshua Richardson (6)
Greyfriars Primary School, King's Lynn

Owen

O wen likes oranges
W aiting in the shop
E ating is fun
N ever eats peas.

Owen Banyard (7)
Greyfriars Primary School, King's Lynn

My First Acrostic - Norfolk & Suffolk

Chloe

C an be happy
H orse lover and horse rider
L ike Elliott
O range juice
E ating apples.

Chloe Bullen (6)
Greyfriars Primary School, King's Lynn

Jack

J oggy
A pple eater
C ake lover
K ind.

Jack Flett (7)
Greyfriars Primary School, King's Lynn

My First Acrostic - Norfolk & Suffolk

Alfie

A dimsin is my best friend
L ike TV
F riendly
I like to play on my Wii
E ggs are nice.

Alfie Crown (7)
Greyfriars Primary School, King's Lynn

Taylor

T ree lover
A pple lover
Y oyo liker
L olly lover
O range fun
R ipe bananas.

Taylor Everitt (7)
Greyfriars Primary School, King's Lynn

My First Acrostic - Norfolk & Suffolk

Charlotte

C ake is yummy
H aving fun
A nice bath
R ed apples are yummy
L ollies are nice
O ranges are juicy
T racing paper is fun
T oo much nice food
E lly the hamster is nice.

Charlotte Colclough (6)
Greyfriars Primary School, King's Lynn

Gabrielle

G iggles sometimes
A scary dream
B ananas
R ed juicy apple
I have friends
E veryone is kind to me
L ovely
L emons
E veryone is lovely.

Gabrielle Colclough (6)
Greyfriars Primary School, King's Lynn

My First Acrostic - Norfolk & Suffolk

Saffron

S ometimes tidy my room
A lways likes apples and oranges
F riendly and kind
F ast runner
R eally good friend
O range is my favourite colour
N ot a very good climber.

Saffron Swalwell (6)
Greyfriars Primary School, King's Lynn

Adele

- A pple liker
- D uck liker
- E aster liker
- L ove sweets
- E aster hunt hide liker.

Adele Eke (7)
Greyfriars Primary School, King's Lynn

My First Acrostic - Norfolk & Suffolk

Isabel

I love ice creams
S illy sometimes
A pple eater
B rave
E ater
L over.

Isabel Overton (7)
Greyfriars Primary School, King's Lynn

Briony

B right
R eally kind
I like pasta
O nly tidy my room if I am in a good mood
N ice
Y ell.

Briony Benjamin (7)
Greyfriars Primary School, King's Lynn

… My First Acrostic - Norfolk & Suffolk

Alice

A lways kind
L icking lollipops
I ce cream lover
C olourful
E ating ice cream.

Alice Zelepukina (6)
Greyfriars Primary School, King's Lynn

Alice

A pple eater
L oves my mum and dad
I ce cream eater
C ream is nice, I guess so
E veryone likes me.

Alice Middleton-Jones (6)
Greyfriars Primary School, King's Lynn

My First Acrostic - Norfolk & Suffolk

Alicia

A lways
L aughs a lot
I like chocolate
C olourful
I like Maisy
A good friend.

Alicia Rolfe (6)
Greyfriars Primary School, King's Lynn

Riley

R eally silly sometimes
I ce in his drink
L olly eater
E njoys school
Y ells at his parents.

Riley Berycz (6)
Greyfriars Primary School, King's Lynn

My First Acrostic - Norfolk & Suffolk

Rebecca

R uns
E ats
B ouncy
E ats eggs
C arrot lover
C ake lover
A nimal lover.

Rebecca Ward (7)
Greyfriars Primary School, King's Lynn

Erin

E ats ice cream
R uns quite fast
I like friends
N ice and shares.

Erin Lanchester (6)
Greyfriars Primary School, King's Lynn

My First Acrostic - Norfolk & Suffolk

Ellie And Easter

E llie is a
L ittle girl
L azy
I am nice
E ats eggs.

E aster chicks
A re funny
S mall Easter eggs
T he
E aster
R abbit.

Ellie-Mai Crawford (6)
Meadow CP School, Lowestoft

Sarah And Sassie

S miling all the time
A dorable
R osy cheeks
A ccident prone
H elpful at home.

S assie is my cat
A dorable
S assie moans all the time
S assie is cheeky
I love Sassie, she
E ats human food.

Sarah Beattie (7)
Meadow CP School, Lowestoft

My First Acrostic - Norfolk & Suffolk

Tayla And Easter

T he good girl
A live
Y oung
L ittle
A nd cool.

E aster eggs
A re delicious
S mall eggs
T hey are sweet
E ggs are made of chocolate
R eally exciting.

Tayla Hayward (6)
Meadow CP School, Lowestoft

Emma And Monkey

E njoy school and
M ilk
M y mum is
A lovely lady.

M onkeys are funny
O n the branch
N aughty too. They have
K urly tails
E ach one is funny
Y ou are my favourite animal.

Emma Henwood (7)
Meadow CP School, Lowestoft

My First Acrostic - Norfolk & Suffolk

Eleanor And Fish

E xciting all the time
L istens well in maths
E ntertaining everyone
A dorable my mum thinks
N early perfect in class
O mnivore because I eat everything
R eally cool I am.

F ish blow bubbles
I n the sea
S he has beautiful shimmering scales
H appily she swims quickly.

Eleanor Manning (6)
Meadow CP School, Lowestoft

Tegan And Dinosaur

T idy
E ats anything
G ood
A fraid
N ice.

D inosaurs lived long ago
I nteresting
N ow they are not alive
O mnivore eats anything
S tomping really hard
A re enormous
U gly dinosaurs
R eally big teeth.

Tegan Arlow (7)
Meadow CP School, Lowestoft

My First Acrostic - Norfolk & Suffolk

Amy And Easter

A dorable
M um loves me
Y oghurt eater.

E aster chicks
A re on my head
S itting on my foot
T ickling me
E verywhere yellow chicks
R unning around.

Amy Clark (6)
Meadow CP School, Lowestoft

Callum And Parrot

C ool
A nnoying
L ittle boy
L azy
U nderstanding
M oaner.

P arrots are noisy
A ll the time
R acing around
R epeating words
O n and on
T alking and screaming.

Callum Westphal (7)
Meadow CP School, Lowestoft

My First Acrostic - Norfolk & Suffolk

Wilym And Racing

W aiting
I nteresting
L ovely
Y oung
M an.

R acing cars are fast
A ll the time
C ars are cool
I like bangers
N early perfect
G reat.

Wilym Dunnell (6)
Meadow CP School, Lowestoft

Sophie And Dinosaur

S miley
O ver good
P recious
H appy
I nteresting
E ats apples.

D angerous
I
N ever go near
O h
S o silly
A re
U
R eally dangerous?

Sophie Bush (6)
Meadow CP School, Lowestoft

My First Acrostic - Norfolk & Suffolk

Natalie And School

N ice all the time
A nd happy
T alented
A nd good
L oves my mum
I love Alexander
E at my tea.

S chool is
C ool
H omework is fun
O bjects are fun to play with
O n the playground
L ove school.

Natalie Raven (6)
Meadow CP School, Lowestoft

Riley And Shark

R unning machine
I ce cream
L ion killing machine
E ye taker
Y oung boy

S ome sharks are swimming in the ocean
H unters are coming for the shark
A ll the sharks swim away
R ace to kill
K ill the shark.

Riley Higgins (7)
Meadow CP School, Lowestoft

My First Acrostic - Norfolk & Suffolk

Kensey And Cat

K ind girl
E xplains nicely
N ice girl
S hares things
E xtra special
Y oung and kind

C urls up
A nd sleeps in
T he bed.

Kensey Wigg (7)
Meadow CP School, Lowestoft

Morgan And Fish

M eadow is my school
O bey your teacher
R unning machine
G reat at football
A lways nice every day
N ever pushing in the line.

F lipping fins
I n a fish tank
S wimming fast
H appy friendly fish.

Morgan Gallagher (7)
Meadow CP School, Lowestoft

My First Acrostic - Norfolk & Suffolk

Annie And Shark

A good time girl
N ice at home
N ot nasty at school
I ce cream eater
E xplains well

S cares you a lot
H as lots of sharp teeth
A ngry shark
R acing other sharks
K ill other fish.

Annie Angus (7)
Meadow CP School, Lowestoft

Isabel And Tiger

I ce cream is my favourite
S chool is the best
A lways happy
B est friend
E ver
L ike a cuddly bear.

T errible
I n the
G arden
E ating
R ed roses.

Isabel Fields (7)
Meadow CP School, Lowestoft

My First Acrostic - Norfolk & Suffolk

Abbie And Dog

A lone
B eautiful
B ike rider
I mportant girl
E xcellent maker of cards.

M akes dog noises like this *woof, woof.*
Y awns very loudly.

D ribbles on the floor.
O nly allowed on the floor.
G ood at cleaning my mum's feet.

B rown as chocolate
O nly eats cat food
E veryone's favourite pet.

Abbie-Beth Beharier (7)
Meadow CP School, Lowestoft

Megan And Tinkerbell

M usic lover
E xtra homework girl
G ood giver, golden girl
A nnoying
N oisy with music.

T inkerbell is a very big dog
I t annoys me
N oisy dog called Tinkerbell
K icks me with her back legs if she doesn't want to go on her lead
E xcellent at breaking out of the fence
R eally wrecks the garden
B all; she loves to play ball
E xcellent at dancing with me
L ikes to chase me.

Megan Sampson (7)
Meadow CP School, Lowestoft

My First Acrostic - Norfolk & Suffolk

Rebecca And Dog

R ainbow loving
E xcellent effort at work
B anana eater
E xplains work well
C ake loving
C astle fabulous
A nimal loving.

D igging machine
O at eater, *mmm*
G ood to be a dog.

Rebecca Casbolt (7)
Meadow CP School, Lowestoft

Neo And Liverpool

N ice
E nemy
O ften

L ove the team
I 'm a big fan of Liverpool
V ery good
E arn lots of money
R ooney was not good enough to play in Liverpool
P oor Gerrard
O beyed the ref
O nly the best team
L ampard doesn't play for that team.

Neo Beck (7)
Meadow CP School, Lowestoft

My First Acrostic - Norfolk & Suffolk

Springtime

S unflowers
P ink blossom
R ed roses
I nteresting seeds
N ests
G od.

William Parsons (5)
Ipswich Preparatory School, Ipswich

Springtime

S unny
P ink blossom
R abbits
I nteresting animals
N ests
G od.

Caitlin Wood (4)
Ipswich Preparatory School, Ipswich

My First Acrostic - Norfolk & Suffolk

Springtime

S pring
P retty flowers
R ain
I nteresting Easter eggs
N ests
G reen.

Naomi De Silva (5)
Ipswich Preparatory School, Ipswich

Springtime

S unflowers

P lants

R ain

I nteresting insects

N ew chicks

G reen.

Jy Naha (4)
Ipswich Preparatory School, Ipswich

My First Acrostic - Norfolk & Suffolk

Springtime

S pring
P ink blossom
R oses
I nteresting rabbits
N ests
G ardening chair.

Lucy Procter (5)
Ipswich Preparatory School, Ipswich

Springtime

- **S** un
- **P** retty bluebells
- **R** abbits
- **I** nsects
- **N** ew animals
- **G** od.

George Lewis (4)
Ipswich Preparatory School, Ipswich

My First Acrostic - Norfolk & Suffolk

Springtime

S pring
P lanting
R abbits
I nteresting snowdrops
N ests
G od.

Angus Williams (5)
Ipswich Preparatory School, Ipswich

Springtime

S pring
P ink blossom
R abbits
I nteresting blossom
N ests
G od.

Monty Brown (5)
Ipswich Preparatory School, Ipswich

My First Acrostic - Norfolk & Suffolk

Springtime

S unflowers
P lants
R abbits
I nteresting flowers
N ew chicks
G od.

Laura Tickle (4)
Ipswich Preparatory School, Ipswich

Springtime

S un
P lants
R abbits
I nteresting blossom
N ests
G arden.

Harry Budd (5)
Ipswich Preparatory School, Ipswich

My First Acrostic - Norfolk & Suffolk

Springtime

S pring
P lants
R abbits
I nteresting daffodils
N ew chicks
G od.

Jensen Hoole (5)
Ipswich Preparatory School, Ipswich

Springtime

- **S** un
- **P** lants
- **R** ain
- **I** nteresting animals
- **N** ests
- **G** od.

Thomas Licence (5)
Ipswich Preparatory School, Ipswich

My First Acrostic - Norfolk & Suffolk

Springtime

S un
P ink blossom
R oses
I nteresting flowers
N ests
G od.

Lia Fletcher (4)
Ipswich Preparatory School, Ipswich

Springtime

S un
P uppies
R abbits
I ncredible
N ew life
G rass.

Charlotte Pudney (4)
Ipswich Preparatory School, Ipswich

My First Acrostic - Norfolk & Suffolk

Springtime

S unglasses
P uppies
R ainbows
I nteresting
N ests
G arden.

Varun Sharma (5)
Ipswich Preparatory School, Ipswich

Springtime

S un
P iglets
R abbits
I nteresting
N ests
G arden.

Maddison Taylor (5)
Ipswich Preparatory School, Ipswich

My First Acrostic - Norfolk & Suffolk

Springtime

S un
P icnics
R ainbows
I ncredible
N ests
G rowing.

Adam Rudolph (5)
Ipswich Preparatory School, Ipswich

Springtime

- **S** un
- **P** etals
- **R** ainbows
- **I** ncredible
- **N** ests
- **G** ardens.

Matthew Daly (4)
Ipswich Preparatory School, Ipswich

My First Acrostic - Norfolk & Suffolk

Springtime

S unglasses
P ink blossom
R unning
I ncredible
N ests
G rowing.

Brylle Ibasco (4)
Ipswich Preparatory School, Ipswich

Springtime

S nowdrops
P ink blossom
R ainbows
I nteresting
N ice weather
G arden.

Joella Kajoba (5)
Ipswich Preparatory School, Ipswich

My First Acrostic - Norfolk & Suffolk

Springtime

S un
P ink
R aindrops
I nsects
N ests
G rowing.

Harvey Ormes (5)
Ipswich Preparatory School, Ipswich

Springtime

- **S** nowdrops
- **P** etals
- **R** abbits
- **I** nsects
- **N** ests
- **G** arden.

Etiane Cheung (4)
Ipswich Preparatory School, Ipswich

My First Acrostic - Norfolk & Suffolk

Springtime

S un
P uppies
R ainbows
I nteresting
N ests
G ardens.

Toby Jermyn (5)
Ipswich Preparatory School, Ipswich

Springtime

S nowdrops
P iglets
R ainbows
I nsects
N est
G arden.

Joshua Midwood (5)
Ipswich Preparatory School, Ipswich

My First Acrostic - Norfolk & Suffolk

Springtime

S nails
P etals
R ainbows
I nsects
N ests
G arden.

Joseph Breheny (4)
Ipswich Preparatory School, Ipswich

Springtime

S nowdrops

P uppies

R abbits

I ncredible

N ests

G arden.

Bethan Cherry (5)
Ipswich Preparatory School, Ipswich

My First Acrostic - Norfolk & Suffolk

Springtime

S un hats
P ink blossom
R ainbows
I nteresting
N ice weather
G arden.

Megan Bureau (5)
Ipswich Preparatory School, Ipswich

Spring

S pring is on its way
P eeping shoots come out in the day
R ain comes sometimes
I t's not here all the time
N o snow
G etting close to summer.

Alexander Mair (5)
Ipswich Preparatory School, Ipswich

My First Acrostic - Norfolk & Suffolk

Spring

S pring is here at last!
P eople are happy
R ain has past
I n my garden I have bugs
N ice spring nights
G eese are flying in the sky.

Eve McCallum (5)
Ipswich Preparatory School, Ipswich

Spring

S pring is hot
P lease give us spring every day
R ain, rain, we need rain for the flowers
I 'll always have to water the flowers
N ext day the beautiful flowers open
G row bigger and bigger.

Helena Marfoh-Gillings (5)
Ipswich Preparatory School, Ipswich

My First Acrostic - Norfolk & Suffolk

Spring

S pringtime is coming
P urple petals on a flower
R ain on petals
I rises grow in the rain
N early summer
G orgeous and wonderful flowers grow.

Muskaan Sethi (6)
Ipswich Preparatory School, Ipswich

Spring

S pring is beautiful, the leaves fall off the trees
P ea pods grow in the spring
R ed tulips grow in spring
I nsects come out in spring
N ow it is springtime
G et ready for spring.

Charlie Parsons (5)
Ipswich Preparatory School, Ipswich

My First Acrostic - Norfolk & Suffolk

Spring

S ky is blue
P lant a flower
R ain go away
I n the shade
N ight flight
G ames day.

Harry Dunnett (5)
Ipswich Preparatory School, Ipswich

Spring

S pring sunshine
P ink flowers
R ain dribbles down from the sky
I like the blossom
N ine fabulous flowers
G ardens are cute and colourful.

Sophie Reeves-Croft (6)
Ipswich Preparatory School, Ipswich

My First Acrostic - Norfolk & Suffolk

Spring

S pring and sun
P ansies and petals
R ain and red tulips
I n the spring insects come out
N ine flowers in a row
G rass to cut.

Harry Roper (5)
Ipswich Preparatory School, Ipswich

Spring

S un is bright
P etals come out
R ed flowers come out
I n the spring blossom comes out
N ight is later
G ardens have flowers.

Samuel Burgoyne (6)
Ipswich Preparatory School, Ipswich

My First Acrostic - Norfolk & Suffolk

Anna

A lways nice
N oisy Anna
N aughty at home
A mazing at climbing.

Anna Van Staden (6)
Ipswich Preparatory School, Ipswich

James

J okes I like
A mazing boy
M y eyes are brown
E very Wednesday I go swimming
S ister called Catherine.

James Whittle (6)
Ipswich Preparatory School, Ipswich

My First Acrostic - Norfolk & Suffolk

Oliver

O ften I go to school
L ook I am in the playground
I have a brother
V ery sporty
E very day I watch TV
R unning is my favourite sport.

Oliver O'Brien (6)
Ipswich Preparatory School, Ipswich

Francesca

F unny Francesca
R oses are my favourite flowers
A mazing blonde hair
N oisy person
C lever girl
E xciting me
S weets I eat
C ats I love
A lways right.

Francesca Rogers (6)
Ipswich Preparatory School, Ipswich

My First Acrostic - Norfolk & Suffolk

Charlie

C lever clogs
H appy boy
A m a good boy at school
R ed is my favourite colour
L ive in my house
I am a new man
E xcellent Charlie.

Charlie Coe (6)
Ipswich Preparatory School, Ipswich

Joe

J olly
O n my face are freckles
E very Sunday I play Lego Batman.

Joseph Christie (6)
Ipswich Preparatory School, Ipswich

My First Acrostic - Norfolk & Suffolk

Sophie

S chool is wonderful
O n Friday I like going to the shops
P retty Sophie
H ug my teddy
I am a mammal
E very day I play with my toys.

Sophie Garner (5)
Ipswich Preparatory School, Ipswich

Tabitha

T he house is always quiet
A mazing me
B ossy boots I am
I have freckles on my nose
T ell me a story
H ard worker
A t school I work all day.

Tabitha Creed (5)
Ipswich Preparatory School, Ipswich

My First Acrostic - Norfolk & Suffolk

Francis

F or lunch I like fish and chips
R unning in the garden
A rmy I love
N aughty Francis in reception
C ranes I like
I have blue eyes
S chool is fun.

Francis Gorham (6)
Ipswich Preparatory School, Ipswich

Samuel

- **S** leepy at school
- **A** rmy is my favourite thing
- **M** y toys are cars
- **U** p the mountains I like skiing
- **E** xcellent boy
- **L** ovely Sam.

Samuel Duncombe (6)
Ipswich Preparatory School, Ipswich

My First Acrostic - Norfolk & Suffolk

William

W ill is funny
I am clever
L azy
L aser Quest
I don't like tennis
A mazing me
M y eyes are blue and I have two pupils.

William Reed (6)
Ipswich Preparatory School, Ipswich

Oliver

O ne brother called Daniel
L ovely me
I am very kind to people
V ery kind me
E xciting school
R ed is my favourite colour.

Oliver Cook (5)
Ipswich Preparatory School, Ipswich

My First Acrostic - Norfolk & Suffolk

Spring

S hoots sprout
P ansies come
R ain falls
I n the spring
N ight comes
G et ready for summer.

Tom Conway (6)
Ipswich Preparatory School, Ipswich

Spring

S pring I love
P ick petals
R ain comes, not very much
I n spring flowers come
N ine daffodils
G ive spring a cheer.

Aiden Pearson (5)
Ipswich Preparatory School, Ipswich

My First Acrostic - Norfolk & Suffolk

Spring

S ky is blue
P ink blossom is appearing
R ains sometimes
I n spring it could be sunny
N ight is wonderful
G ardens are full of tulips.

Ryan Goodarzi (6)
Ipswich Preparatory School, Ipswich

Eco Warriors

E nergy helps you to run around
C an we please compost?
O nly eat healthy food

W ater your plants
A nd please keep our world tidy
R ecycle cardboard
R ubbish in your bin could be recycled
I 'm environmentally friendly
O ur world needs care
R ight now
S how we care.

Rosie Valentine (7)
Langham Village School, Norfolk

My First Acrostic - Norfolk & Suffolk

Eco Warrior

E ach day I go to a sol plant
C ompost every day
O rganise a composting club

W ater your plants
A lways turn the tap off
R emember to look after our world
R emind people to switch the TV off
I use solar panels
O ur planet needs you
R euse, recycle all the time
S top the planet from destruction.

Teddy Valentine (7)
Langham Village School, Norfolk

Eco Warriors

E co
C ompost carrots
O nly eat healthy food

W ater mustn't be wasted
A lways save electricity
R ubbish in the bin
R ain water in the butt
I always save energy
O ur world needs care
R aise monkeys from the trees
S ave the world.

Connor McInally (7)
Langham Village School, Norfolk

My First Acrostic - Norfolk & Suffolk

Eco Warriors

E nvironments are beautiful
C reatures in the compost bin
O ak trees blowing in the wind

W alk to stay fit and grow flowers
A gain and again water your plants
R ecycle things like
R ubbish
I n this world don't throw things away
O ur world needs to be good
R ubbish in the recycle bin
S o you have to care.

Lily Everard (7)
Langham Village School, Norfolk

Eco Warriors

E at healthy food.
C ompost food which you don't eat and bins of food
O nly eat the good food for you 5 times a day like fruit

W asting food is bad
A fter you recycle things wash your hands.
R aise money for school
R ecycle the foods in bins.
I save money for the poor people around the world
O ur world needs more care
R aining is good for flowers
S ave energy.

Bethany Everitt (7)
Langham Village School, Norfolk

My First Acrostic - Norfolk & Suffolk

Eco Warrior

E nvironments are good for birds.
C ompost all your cardboard.
O rganise your compost greens.

W ater is good for the environment.
A lways switch off the tap.
R emember to switch off the cooker.
R ecycle your rubbish.
I always put my rubbish in the bin.
O ur world must stay green.
R ain is good for compost.

Maisie Moxon (6)
Langham Village School, Norfolk

Eco Warriors

E co
C ompost plant waste
O nly recycle healthy waste

W aste food goes in the composting bin
A ir needs to be fresh
R ecycle rubbish
R ubbish goes in the bin
I t is important to look after the world
O ur world needs help
R ight now
S ave the world.

Blue Wilson (7)
Langham Village School, Norfolk

My First Acrostic - Norfolk & Suffolk

Erin's Little Poem

E ager, terrific little girl
R ound the bend
I n the box
N o bags in a car

P in down the ghost
A ttack the dragon
I 'm sick on my bed
N ow my bed is covered in flowers.

Erin Pain (5)
Middleton CP School, Middleton

My Work Is Lovely

I like to play with a car
And I like myself
Naughty boy!

Silly Billy
I can be a little
Mouse skipping and jumping around the house
Pets at the door
Shh, don't wake the baby
Over and over I play inside
No Ian, go to sleep!

Ian Simpson (6)
Middleton CP School, Middleton

My First Acrostic - Norfolk & Suffolk

Saffron's Poem

S uper every day
A musing to my cuddly toy
F affy sometimes when I'm cross
F unny to my friends
R avenous when it's lunchtime
O lives are disgusting
N ice to my friends.

Saffron Jackson (6)
Middleton CP School, Middleton

My Funny Things

D reaming in my bed
A nts in my pants
V oice shouting, screaming
I like playing on my bike
D isturbing nt sister in her room

L ots of love for my mummy
L ittle bones round the house
O h I forgot my drink for my lunch
Y ummy yoghurt for my tummy
D ancing to music.

David Lloyd (6)
Middleton CP School, Middleton

My First Acrostic - Norfolk & Suffolk

Thomas' Poem

T errific at maths
H elping people
O ver the river
M oving fast
A mazing work
S uper at reading

M aths I love
A ngry at people when they annoy me
R ed pandas are my favourite mammal
S leepy to not get to school
H appy when I make things
A nd eyes are green
L azy so I can read Astrix
L ate to school.

Thomas Marshall (6)
Middleton CP School, Middleton

Hebe's Poem

Hairdresser, I want to cut my hair, oh yeah!
Eat, eat, I love food, nobody loves it except me.
Blue, my favourite colour is blue, I love the colour blue.
Enchanted, I am the enchanted girl in the land.

Cooking, oh cooking, I love cooking.
Olympic games, I practise for the Olympic games.
On task, I am on task whenever I go to school.
Kite, oh my kite, I have got a new one in my box.
Excellent, I am excellent in the whole entire world.

Hebe Cooke (6)
Middleton CP School, Middleton

My First Acrostic - Norfolk & Suffolk

Layla's Poem

L ight brown is my favourite colour
A pple is my favourite fruit
Y oung is the best
L ight green is my second favourite colour
A pproachable; my friends can talk to me.

B rilliant as a friend
R eally pretty
O n task of writing
W in on sports day
N ervous when I go on stage.

Layla Brown (7)
Middleton CP School, Middleton

Gabriella's Poem

G reat Gab being so generous always
O n task
R emembering to be polite
G iving people back their things when I've borrowed them
E arwigging into other people's conversations
O utwitting other people
U nforgettable little girl
S o lovely

G iggling in class, giggling at home
A ngry at people when they're not being very nice to me
B ye-bye school, hello summer
B eing funny at home and at school
Y ummy, yummy *Gabriella!*

Gabriella Pattinson (7)
Middleton CP School, Middleton

My First Acrostic - Norfolk & Suffolk

The Magnificent Me

C ars are awesome
A mazing and
E xtraordinary
M y favourite chocolate
E asy-going with my mum
R umble in my tum
O lives are disgusting
N ight I like to sleep.

Cameron Berry (7)
Middleton CP School, Middleton

My Life

M agnificently clever
O n task all the time
L ate to school
L aughing, telling jokes like a comedian
I ncredible imagination
E xtraordinary memory

S uper at video games
H ot chilli is my Club Penguin name
A chievement is what I do best
W riting is my hobby.

Mollie Shaw (7)
Middleton CP School, Middleton

My First Acrostic - Norfolk & Suffolk

Todd

T odd always reading
O dd books
D oing odd things
D rawing odd pictures.

Todd Middleton (5)
Redcastle Furze Primary School, Thetford

Kiran

K iran
I s brave
R emembering spellings
A nd learning her numbers
N othing is too hard.

Kiran Manir (6)
Redcastle Furze Primary School, Thetford

My First Acrostic - Norfolk & Suffolk

Alex

A lex
L ikes playing
E ating fruit
X tra nice all the time.

Alex Knock (5)
Redcastle Furze Primary School, Thetford

Paydon

P aydon
A sks questions
Y ou did that, why?
D o you have teeth?
O h, can you help me?
N ever quits.

Paydon Blow (5)
Redcastle Furze Primary School, Thetford

My First Acrostic - Norfolk & Suffolk

Kira

K ira
I s
R eading
A lot of books.

Kira Baumane (5)
Redcastle Furze Primary School, Thetford

Harry

H arry is happy
A lways smiling
R eading books
R unning around
Y es, that's Harry.

Harry Brown (5)
Redcastle Furze Primary School, Thetford

My First Acrostic - Norfolk & Suffolk

Ricardo

R icardo
I s
C ool
A nd
R eady for school
D oing his homework
O nce a day.

Ricardo Da Silva (6)
Redcastle Furze Primary School, Thetford

Bruno

B runo wears his blue jumper
R unning around the playground
U p we go!
N o pushing each other
O r you will be sitting on the wall.

Bruno Cardoso (6)
Redcastle Furze Primary School, Thetford

My First Acrostic - Norfolk & Suffolk

Codie

C odie
O n her bike
D ancing at home
I like doing
E verything.

Codie Ancliff (6)
Redcastle Furze Primary School, Thetford

Katharine

K atharine
A ngel
T elling stories
H appy to colour pictures
A nd
R unning in races
I nterested in films
N ever sad
E njoys playing.

Katharine Mold (6)
Redcastle Furze Primary School, Thetford

My First Acrostic - Norfolk & Suffolk

Natasha

N atasha is
A lways
T hinking
A nd
S wimming and is
H appy eating
A pples.

Natasha Laurie (6)
Redcastle Furze Primary School, Thetford

Andrew

A ndrew
N oisy chatting
D reams in class
R eading
E njoys playing at home
W ith his friends.

Andrew Souness (6)
Redcastle Furze Primary School, Thetford

My First Acrostic - Norfolk & Suffolk

Daniel

D elicious cake I like most.
A ngry with my brother.
N uisance at home.
I mportant things is what I do.
E xciting when playing football.
L azy watching telly.

Daniel Turner (6)
Runcton Holme CE Primary School, Runcton Holme

Lucie

L ucky in love
U gly I am not!
C ute snuggled in my bed
I nterested in my homework
E njoy working at school.

Lucie Canham (6)
Runcton Holme CE Primary School, Runcton Holme

My First Acrostic - Norfolk & Suffolk

Grace

G rateful is what she's like.
R ides a bike but with stabilizers.
A ll my pets love me.
C an do a handstand.
E xcellent at things.

Grace Herbert (5)
Runcton Holme CE Primary School, Runcton Holme

Reece

R uncton Home is my school.
E veryone is my favourite.
E nergetic is what I am.
C urious like a monkey.
E ars let me hear like a dog.

Reece Hockton (6)
Runcton Holme CE Primary School, Runcton Holme

My First Acrostic - Norfolk & Suffolk

Amber

A lways good
M ummy's who I love
B ears are my favourite animals
E nergy I have
R un very fast.

Amber Nederpel (6)
Runcton Holme CE Primary School, Runcton Holme

Emily

E veryone likes me.
M um is my friend.
I n love with a boy.
L ucky for mates.
Y oung and beautiful.

Emily Shimmin (6)
Runcton Holme CE Primary School, Runcton Holme

My First Acrostic - Norfolk & Suffolk

Olivia

O rdinary person with my friends
L ovely like my mum
I live in a house with my family
V ery kind to everyone
I like going to the park
A lways happy and cheerful.

Olivia Ward (6)
Runcton Holme CE Primary School, Runcton Holme

Libby Anna

L ibby met her best friend at the horse's stables.
I like horses, they are my best friends.
B rown and black horses are the best.
B rownies are so cool.
Y our horses are really, really cool.

A nd I love chocolate.
N ay is my horse's name.
N ay is really good.
A nd my horse loves its stables.

Elizabeth Napper (7)
Sacred Heart Convent School, Swaffham

My First Acrostic - Norfolk & Suffolk

Isobel Fifi

I sobel loves dancing
S olo is the way I like
O n my own
B anana yum, you're my best
E mily is one of my friends, I
L ike to do splashes in the water.

F ifi is my auntie
I like my pretty Barbies
F lowers, the smell of flowers
I t is like summertime.

Isobel McPartlin (6)
Sacred Heart Convent School, Swaffham

Emily Alice

Emily looks like Elizabeth.
My best friend is Elizabeth.
In school and everywhere.
Little Tilly is my only sister.
Yo-yos are the best.

A summer's day is my favourite day.
Lazy people I don't like.
I like my little sister she is very
Cute and cuddly.
Elizabeth loves horses.

Emily Harpham-Wells (7)
Sacred Heart Convent School, Swaffham

My First Acrostic - Norfolk & Suffolk

Alice Sarah

A lice loves horses. She
L oves jumping on her horses.
I love playing with my toys.
C ats are everywhere.
E ve is my friend.

S even people are my friends.
A ine is one of my friends.
R oses are my favourite flower.
A lice went horse riding, the
H orse enjoyed it.

Alice Christian (7)
Sacred Heart Convent School, Swaffham

Charlotte

C harlotte is tall
H orses are her favourite things
A nd she likes jumping and cantering
R unning and playing with her big sister
L ucy
O ver tall jumps
T aking part in shows
T rying my best
E veryone is there.

Charlotte MacEwan (6)
Sacred Heart Convent School, Swaffham

My First Acrostic - Norfolk & Suffolk

Áine Julie

A ine likes to play with her Barbie toys.
I like to go to dancing.
N iamh is annoying and she always teases me.
E lizabeth is nice because she is my best friend.

J ulie-Anne is my mum.
U nder my bed are my toys.
L ots of chocolate for me.
I have chocolates on the top of the shelf.
E verybody comes to my birthday party.

Áine Matthews (7)
Sacred Heart Convent School, Swaffham

Skorupi

S corpion-like
K icking
O val eyes
R ipping claws
U nder a rage
P oisonous
I nk colour.

Alexander Wrathall (5)
Tattingstone CE (VCP) School, Tattingstone

My First Acrostic - Norfolk & Suffolk

Aliens

A ntennae
L ight
I nvisible
E normous body
N oisy
S limy.

Michael Vinnicombe (6)
Tattingstone CE (VCP) School, Tattingstone

Flowers

F uschia
L ily
O range
W illow tree
E vergreen
R ose
S unflower.

Lucy Sweeney (6)
Tattingstone CE (VCP) School, Tattingstone

My First Acrostic - Norfolk & Suffolk

Crocus

C rystal
R ose
O rchid
C rocus
U nderground
S oil.

Morgan Porter (6)
Tattingstone CE (VCP) School, Tattingstone

Truck

Trains
Road
Unload
Carry
Kilos.

Joseph Moore (5)
Tattingstone CE (VCP) School, Tattingstone

My First Acrostic - Norfolk & Suffolk

Flowers

F loppy flowers in the garden
L upins dancing
O rchids standing tall
W allflower in a bed
E vergreen leaves
R oses red
S nowdrops white.

Richard Marsh (6)
Tattingstone CE (VCP) School, Tattingstone

Dinosaur

D irty heels
I ntelligent
N ot nice
O ld dinosaurs
S caly skin
A llosaurus
U gly
R aptor.

Jake Henson (6)
Tattingstone CE (VCP) School, Tattingstone

My First Acrostic - Norfolk & Suffolk

Cats

C lever
A ctive
T ame
S leepy.

Esme Chancellor (5)
Tattingstone CE (VCP) School, Tattingstone

Flower

F lowers bloom like gold.
L ilies smell like a fresh lake.
O rchids dance gently in the breeze
W eeds weaving round trees
E vergreen stays green forever
R oses prick, careful of the rose.

Phoebe Agar (6)
Tattingstone CE (VCP) School, Tattingstone

My First Acrostic - Norfolk & Suffolk

Harry

H appy to help
A ny washing up to do?
R eading is awesome and exciting
R eading is incredible
Y ikes it's a miracle.

L eaping very high, I can jump over fallen trees
E ating a big cake
E ating a large sausage
M eeting with my friends
I ncredible with gadgets
N o one goes in my room
G ladiators in a battle fiercely in a fight.

Harry Leeming (7)
Wenhaston Primary School, Wenhaston

Jamie Lea

J umping on the trampoline very high
A lways helping my mum in the kitchen
M rs Man is my favourite teacher
I t is maths homework tonight
E at up your dinner,' said Mummy.

L eaping high over the tall trees
E ach day I go to the shop
A lways playing with my sister.

S cary, my sister scares me
T ake my dog for a walk
A my is my best friend
C arys always lets me play with her
E xcited when my mum picks up my nan
Y ellow is my favourite colour.

Jamie Lea Stacey (7)
Wenhaston Primary School, Wenhaston

My First Acrostic - Norfolk & Suffolk

George

G eorge likes cricket
E nergetically hitting the ball
O ver the hedge
R unning to the stick and back
G etting 20 runs and getting points
E ating lunch.

C heeky chimpanzee
U nable to lock the door
R unning down the stairs saying, 'Hooligan'
T ugging on my hair
I t's a shark (my brothers)
S nack time.

George Curtis (6)
Wenhaston Primary School, Wenhaston

Jake

Jake is silly
Always messing my hair up
KitKats are the best
Excited because

My dog is coming up the stairs
Cheeky chappy
Mum calls me Monkey
And I laugh
Sweets are the best food I've tasted
Ten fish are in my fish tank
Eating sprinkles of fish food
Relaxed in peace at home.

Jake McMaster (7)
Wenhaston Primary School, Wenhaston

My First Acrostic - Norfolk & Suffolk

Kiaya

K iaya is organised.
I do not like to tidy my room though.
A mazing at maths.
Y apping on the telephone to Nellie.
A ny chance of you coming round?

C heeky chimpanzee,' said my dad.
O ranges give me a headache.
O utside my room on the door it says
K eep out'.
E mma is a good friend to me.

Kiaya Cooke (6)
Wenhaston Primary School, Wenhaston

Olivia

O rganised for school.
L ate for school sometimes.
I nviting girls to my birthday party.
V ery good at spelling.
I ce cream is my favourite food.
A lways do what my parents tell me.

S illy at home sometimes.
M ummy loves me.
I cicles hang from the ceiling.
T ell the truth.
H all is where my party is.
E arly to wake up.
R eally crazy.
S illy girl sometimes.

Olivia Smithers (7)
Wenhaston Primary School, Wenhaston

My First Acrostic - Norfolk & Suffolk

My Crazy Cat

C hews rats and birds
H igh jumping onto the wall
A ches because he runs around all the time
R eal life cat
L icking cat
I love him very much
E ek he is eating cabbage

C urling around with his body
A ttacks! He creeps up to the cat
T ackling Jack's cat.

Bethany Constance (6)
Yoxford Primary School, Yoxford

Ben Likes Me

My cat is called Ben and he eats
Yoghurt!

Crazy cat
Always hungry and miaows
Then he cries to come indoors.

Harry Nichols (7)
Yoxford Primary School, Yoxford

My First Acrostic - Norfolk & Suffolk

Pigeon Words

P ercy shows Polly his bum!
I like pigeons.
G ood flyers.
E very pigeon in the world flies.
O n our school roof they sit.
N ice coloured feathers.

Ryan Southey (6)
Yoxford Primary School, Yoxford

Speed Cars

I like them

L ook out the cars might crash!
I t goes fast when the pedal is down.
K evin goes to watch the drag cars.
E veryone wants to go in the jet car.

C locks can't beat the jet cars
A car skidded because it was going too fast.
R ace that car!
S peed.

Oscar Phillips (6)
Yoxford Primary School, Yoxford

My First Acrostic - Norfolk & Suffolk

Grandad

G reat at games.
R eally fun
A nd he likes the cats
N ice to me.
D oesn't know everything
A nd he sorts out problems.
D angerous sometimes when he's naughty.

Maisie Beckett (6)
Yoxford Primary School, Yoxford

Cuddly Mum

Mummy loves me.
Yes she takes me to school.

My mummy is lovely and cuddly
Up the road we go to school
My mum kisses me goodbye!

Jaydon Johnson (5)
Yoxford Primary School, Yoxford

My First Acrostic - Norfolk & Suffolk

My Best Friend

Daisy is my cocker spaniel.
And she loves to play ball.
I like her.
She chases bad animals away.
You are cuddly with soft fur.

Daisy loves her bed.
On the sofa she jumps.
Good dog.

Cameron Cutler (5)
Yoxford Primary School, Yoxford

Zac The Boy

My brother is called Zac.
Yes I love him.

Bikes are fun when we play
In the garden.
Good things to do with Zac.

Beach walking,
Running and playing,
Other things to do.
Tree climbing on our tree house.
He helps me tidy my bedroom
Every day.
Rugby is good as well.

Luke Clarke (5)
Yoxford Primary School, Yoxford

My First Acrostic - Norfolk & Suffolk

Blossom The Cat

B lossom likes chasing rats
L ike my bed because it is soft
O ver the fence there was a dog
S he is sweet
S he likes me because she sits on my lap
O n the holidays I play in the garden
M y cat is lovely.

Jacob Last (7)
Yoxford Primary School, Yoxford

Lovely Family

My mummy likes to go on the computer.
Unbelievable because she gives me presents.
Mummy likes the news and the weather.
Most days she eats potatoes.
Yesterday she gave me a hug.

Dylan Corbett (6)
Yoxford Primary School, Yoxford

My First Acrostic - Norfolk & Suffolk

Young Writers Information

We hope you have enjoyed reading this book - and that you will continue to enjoy it in the coming years.

If you like reading and writing poetry drop us a line, or give us a call, and we'll send you a free information pack.

Alternatively if you would like to order further copies of this book or any of our other titles, then please give us a call or log onto our website at www.youngwriters.co.uk.

Young Writers Information
Remus House
Coltsfoot Drive
Peterborough
PE2 9JX
(01733) 890066